Why Must I..

Eat Healthy Food?

Jackie Gaff

**Photography by
Chris Fairclough**

CHERRYTREE BOOKS

Planned and produced by Discovery Books Ltd
Editor: Helena Attlee
Designer: Ian Winton
Illustrator: Joanna Williams

Consultant: Pat Jackson, Professional Officer for School Nursing, The Community Practitioners' and
Health Visitors' Association.

Acknowledgments
The author and publisher would like to thank the following for kind permission to reproduce photographs:
Corbis: page 8 (Gareth Brown/Corbis), page 16 (Jennie Woodcock; Reflections Photolibrary/Corbis),
page 23 (Jean-Yves Ruszniewski; Tempsport/Corbis); Getty Images: page 29 (The Image Bank); Science
Photo Library: page 4 (Alfred Pasieka/SPL).
Commissioned photography by Chris Fairclough.

The author, packager, and publisher would like to thank the following people for their participation in
the book: Alice Baldwin-Hay, Heather and William Cooper and Ieuan Crowe.

Contents

Why Must I Eat Healthy Food?

If you eat healthy food, your body will be healthy, too. Food is the fuel that gives you energy.

Your body needs food to make and mend **cells**. You have skin cells and muscle cells, bone cells and blood cells — every single part of you is made up of its own kind of cells.

Food is the fuel that gives you energy for everything you do.

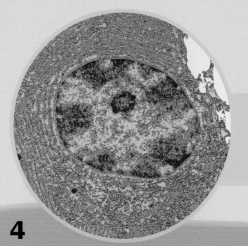

The cells that make up all the different bits of your body are too small to see. This picture of a human cell was taken under a **microscope**.

Food factories

Your body cannot make its own food. Only plants can do this. They take water and other **nutrients** from the soil, and a gas called carbon dioxide from the air. Then they use the energy in sunlight to turn them into food.

Healthy food gives your body the energy for mending everything, from cuts and scrapes to broken bones.

Your body burns food fuel all the time, even when you are sitting still!

Whether you are asleep or awake, the fuel that keeps you alive and healthy comes from your food.

Let's Eat

Your body has a built-in alarm clock. When you feel hungry, you know it's time to eat.

Being really hungry can sometimes give you a stomachache.

A healthy breakfast and a glass of juice are a good start to the day.

To stay full of food fuel, your body needs three good meals a day — breakfast, lunch, and dinner.

It doesn't matter too much what you eat and drink at each meal, as long as each day's meals add up to a **balanced diet.**

HEALTHY HINTS

- **Try to have breakfast soon after you get up.**

- **Eat three good meals each day.**

- **Do not eat a snack just before a meal.**

It is all right to snack if you get hungry during the day, but try to choose something healthy.

A banana makes a healthy, filling snack.

Down the Hatch

Chopping and mashing, squeezing and churning — your body has to work like a kitchen blender every time you eat.

The way your body breaks food down is called **digestion.**

It starts in your mouth, when your teeth chop each mouthful into a soft, mushy mixture.

Babies do not have many teeth. They can only eat food that has already been mashed up.

When you swallow your food, it goes down a tube to your stomach. This tube is called the **esophagus**.

Your stomach churns the food mixture around until it is all runny, like soup.

HEALTHY HINTS

- **Help your digestion — chew your food thoroughly before you swallow it.**

When the food is runny enough, it is pushed out of your stomach into the **intestines**. This is where your body takes the nutrients that it needs out of the food.

Waste Not, Want Not

The intestine is the long tube that joins your stomach to your bottom.

The first part of it is called the small intestine. The lower part of the tube is called the large intestine.

In the small intestine, the food you eat is broken down into even smaller bits. The important nutrients from the food then pass through the wall of the intestine and are **absorbed** into your blood vessels.

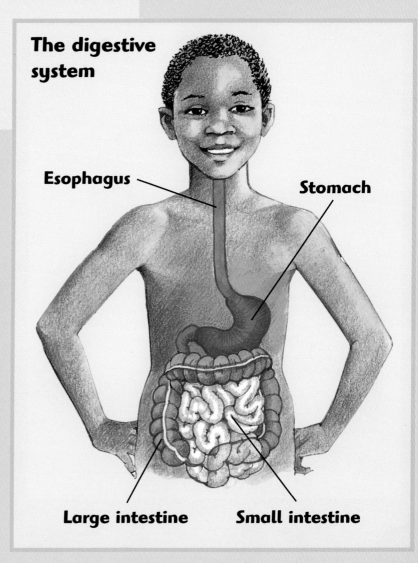

The digestive system

Esophagus

Stomach

Large intestine

Small intestine

Fruit is full of **fiber**. Fiber helps food to move smoothly through the intestine.

Some food cannot be digested. It passes into the large intestine. Your body gets rid of this leftover food, or waste, when you go to the bathroom.

HEALTHY HINTS

- **Eat plenty of fruit and vegetables.**

- **Always remember to wash your hands after you go to the bathroom.**

Don't forget! Wash the **germs** off your hands after you go to the bathroom.

Getting at Goodness

Whether it's an apple or a chunk of cheese, every kind of food has some kind of nutrients in it.

There are six main kinds of nutrients — water, **carbohydrates**, **fats**, **proteins**, **minerals**, and **vitamins**. Your body uses some to get energy, and others to make and mend cells.

Night vision

Carrots really do help you see in the dark! They're packed with vitamin A, which plays a big part in helping your eyes deal with changes in light levels.

Water is a very important nutrient. Without it, your body couldn't turn other food nutrients into energy.

Your blood is a watery river that flows around your body, carrying all sorts of nutrients to your cells.

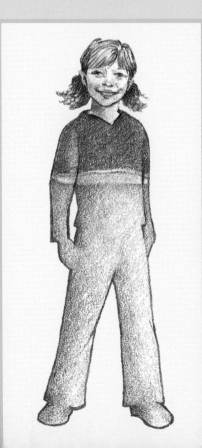

Most of your body (blue in this picture) is made up of water.

Make sure you drink plenty of water.

Energy Food

Do you keep running out of steam? You may be eating the wrong things!

Your body gets most of its energy from the two kinds of carbohydrate — sugars and **starches**.

Most sweet-tasting food has sugar in it, but the healthiest source of sugar is fruit.

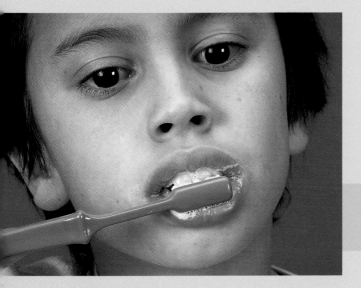

Try to brush your teeth as soon as you can after eating sugary food.

Sugars are digested more quickly and easily than starches. That means sugars give you a quick burst of energy, while starches last the distance.

So, if you keep running out of steam, you probably need to eat more starches.

Starchy foods include bread, cereal, rice, and pasta.

Vitamin C

Fruit is a great source of vitamin C. Vitamin C helps to keep your gums and teeth healthy, and your bones and muscles strong. It also helps your body fight off illness.

Fatty Facts

You need to eat a bit of fatty food, but too much of it is bad for you.

The trouble with food that contains lots of fat and sugar is that it tastes so good. If you eat too much, your body will store up fat, and you will put on weight.

Eating too much fat when you are young can lead to illnesses such as heart disease when you are older.

Save very sweet foods like cakes and cookies for special occasions.

Hamburgers contain lots of fat, so don't eat them too often.

Cookies and potato chips taste great, but they are full of sugar and fat. Make them an extra special treat by not eating them too often.

Eating too much sugar is bad for you in other ways as well. Sugar can also damage your teeth.

HEALTHY HINTS

- Try not to eat extra-fatty food such as potato chips and fries.

Body-building Food

Your body needs proteins to make everything from muscle and bone cells, to heart and lung cells.

You also need proteins to keep your various body parts in good working order and to mend them if they are damaged.

We all have accidents. Your body would not be able to heal cuts and scrapes without proteins.

You need to eat quite a lot of protein every day, but don't worry, there's plenty of food to choose from. Protein foods include meat, fish, beans, nuts, eggs, milk, and cheese.

Nuts make a healthy, protein-packed snack. But beware, some people are **allergic** to nuts.

Dairy products such as milk, cheese, and butter are good sources of protein.

Vitamin D

Milk, eggs, and tuna are rich in proteins. They are a great source of the vitamin that helps keep your bones and teeth healthy — vitamin D.

Keeping a Balance

How would you like to eat nothing but pasta every day for breakfast, lunch, and dinner?

Eating the same things all the time isn't just boring, it's unhealthy.

Healthy eating means eating lots of different food, so you get lots of different nutrients.

The food pyramid makes balancing your daily diet simple. The foods you need to eat are toward the bottom. The foods you only need a little of are right at the very top.

Candies, chips and other **junk food** have few of the really useful vitamins and minerals. Instead, they have lots of fat, sugar, and salt, which your body can easily get too much of.

If you take a packed lunch to school, try to fill your lunchbox with healthy, nutritious things.

Healthy snacks are better for you, and they will give you more energy.

HEALTHY HINTS

- Balance your daily diet by eating lots of different foods.

- Try not to eat junk food, but if you can't stay away from it, only eat it every now and then.

21

Measuring Up

The energy that keeps your body running comes from carbohydrates, fats, and protein.

Scientists use units called **calories** to measure the energy in food. Every gram of carbohydrate has four calories. So does every gram of protein. But every gram of fat has nine calories.

It's easy to eat too many calories. Your body stores leftover calories as body fat.

The carbohydrates in a large apple add up to about 125 calories.

The fat in a single order of fries from a fast-food restaurant adds up to almost twice as many calories as an apple.

You'd have to swim nonstop for about half an hour to burn off the energy in an apple, while it would take almost an hour to burn off the calories in a portion of fries!

HEALTHY HINTS

- Cut down on high-fat meat dishes such as sausages and burgers.

- If food is cooked in fat or oil, only eat a little, every now and then.

Try not to eat too many dairy products, like full-fat cheese.

Weighty Matters

People come in all shapes and sizes.
Some are tall and others are short.
Some are big and others are skinny.

You probably look very like your parents did when they were your age. Body type runs in families, and is passed down through the generations.

It's fun to see how fast you are growing by using a height chart.

Your weight is a balance between the calories you eat and the calories you use to live, move, and grow.

Your weight does not depend only on your height and shape, because some people have heavier bones than others.

The best way for you to keep your weight healthy is to eat a balanced diet and exercise.

Each person has their own healthy weight, which is just right for their age and body type.

HEALTHY HINTS

- **Visit a doctor if you think your weight is unhealthy.**

Food Allergies

Even healthy foods are not good for everyone. There are foods that can make some people very ill indeed.

Their body treats the food like an invading germ and tries to fight it off. When bodies fight food in this way, people are said to have a food allergy.

Some people can't eat anything made from wheat. Others can't eat anything containing cows' milk, like yogurt, milk, and cheese.

A food allergy may make people break out in an itchy **rash**, or their stomach may hurt. A very bad allergy can make their lips, tongue, and throat swell up so that it's difficult to breathe.

Sometimes children grow out of food allergies as they get older. Other allergies may never go away.

HEALTHY HINTS

- **If you think you may have a food allergy, ask your parent or guardian to take you to the doctor.**

- **If you have a food allergy, ask what is in food when you eat at a friend's house or a restaurant.**

Lots of people are allergic to nuts. Say "no thanks" to any food you aren't sure about.

Delicious Tastes

Now you know what food does for your body, don't forget to enjoy it — good food tastes good, as well as doing you good!

Remember that your body uses food for energy. If you are feeling tired, think about what you eat and when you eat it.

Talk to your parent or guardian about the food you eat. Ask for their help in balancing your daily diet.

Do you fill your body up with food fuel three times a day — at breakfast, lunch, and dinner? If you feel hungry between meals, do you choose a healthy snack to keep you going?

Healthy food is delicious, so enjoy it!

Glossary

Absorb
To take something in or to suck it up.

Allergic, Allergy
When someone has an allergy, their body is sensitive to an outside substance and reacts as though it is harmful.

Balanced diet
A balanced diet is one that has the right amounts of all the food nutrients needed to keep your body healthy.

Blood vessel
One of the tubes through which blood flows.

Calorie
A unit for measuring the amount of energy that can be produced from different foods.

Carbohydrate
Carbohydrates are nutrients that provide your body with energy to live, grow and mend itself. There are two main kinds — sugars and starches.

Cell
Cells are the body's building blocks, just as bricks are a house's building blocks.

Diet
The food and drink that you have day by day, and week by week.

Digestion
The process in which your body breaks the food you eat down and takes the nutrients you need from it.

Esophagus
The tube down which food travels from your mouth to your stomach.

Fat
Many foods contain fat. It is important not to eat too much of foods that are very fatty, greasy or oily.

Fiber
Fiber is tough plant material that bodies find hard to digest. Some people call it roughage.

Germ
A tiny living thing that causes disease.

Intestine
Your intestine is the tube through which digested food passes. It starts at your stomach and ends at your bottom.

Junk food
Food with few useful nutrients, but with a lot of fat, sugar, or salt.

Microscope
A device in which lenses are used to magnify objects, making them look bigger.

Minerals
Minerals are substances that are not created by living things. Many minerals are nutrients.

Nutrient
A nutrient is a substance that provides the body with energy or materials to help it live, grow or mend itself.

Protein
Proteins are nutrients that supply you with energy, but their main job is helping your body to build and repair itself.

Rash
Rashes cause tiny, itchy spots on the skin.

Starches
Starches are the carbohydrates found mainly in bread and potatoes.

Sugar
Sugar is a source of energy. But it is also added to food. It is important not to eat too many sweet things.

Vitamin
Vitamins are nutrients which your body needs to change food into energy and to build new cells.

Further Resources

Web Sites

www.bam.gov
The Body and Mind site, run by the Centers for Disease and Prevention, uses a light touch and lively activities to teach children about nutrition.

www.dob5aday.com
Interactive healthy eating web site for children, including games, music, recipes and other activities. Includes pages for children, parents and teachers.

www.kidshealth.org
American, child-centred site devoted to all aspects of health and wellbeing. Includes several pages on healthy eating and recipe ideas.

www.bbc.co.uk/health/nutrition
BBC web site containing articles and news on all aspects of child and adult health, including a section devoted to child nutrition, with advice on healthy eating and suggestions for healthy lunchboxes.

www.foodworks.co.nz
The New Zealand Nutrition Foundation web site, which aims to encourage healthy eating in New Zealand.

www.healthinsite.gov.au
Government-sponsored health site covering a wide range of up-to-date health-related topics. Includes information on young people and obesity, and food allergies.

Books

Lobb, Janice. *At Home With Science: Bump! Thump! How Do We Jump?* Kingfisher, 2000.

Rockwell, Lizzy. *Good Enough to Eat: a Kid's Guide to Food and Nutrition.* HarperCollins, 1999.

Royston, Angela. *Look After Yourself: Healthy Food.* Heinemann Library, 2003.

Royston, Angela. *My Amazing Body: Staying Healthy.* Raintree, 2004.

Ganeri, Anita. *Your Digestive System.* Gareth Stevens, 2003.

Index